Verbs

Kara Murray

PowerKiDS press
New York

Published in 2014 by The Rosen Publishing Group, Inc.
29 East 21st Street, New York, NY 10010

First Edition

Editor: Amelie von Zumbusch
Book Design: Colleen Bialecki

Photo Credits: Cover altrendo images/Stockbyte/Getty Images; p. 4 iStockphoto/Thinkstock; p. 5 Jupiterimages/BananaStock/Thinkstock; p. 7 Cynoclub/Shutterstock.com; p. 8 Elizabeth Marie/Flickr/ Getty Images; p. 10 David De Lossy/Photodisc/Thinkstock; p. 11 Denizo71/Shutterstock.com; p. 13 Ron Embleton/The Bridgeman Art Library/Getty Images; p. 14 TristanBM/Shutterstock.com; p. 17 Jandrie Lombard/Shutterstock.com; p. 18 Image Source/Getty Images; p. 19 Holly Kuchera/Shutterstock.com; p. 20 Jon Feingersh/Blend Images/Getty Images; p. 21 Morgan Lane Photography/Shutterstock.com.

Library of Congress Cataloging-in-Publication Data
Murray, Kara.
  Verbs / By Kara Murray. — First Edition.
      pages cm. — (Core language skills)
  Includes index.
  ISBN 978-1-4777-0801-9 (library binding) — ISBN 978-1-4777-0974-0 (pbk.) —
ISBN 978-1-4777-0975-7 (6-pack)
  1. English language—Verb—Juvenile literature. 2. English language—Parts of speech—Juvenile literature.
  3. English language—Grammar—Juvenile literature. I. Title.
  PE1271.M87 2014
  428.2—dc23
                                                    2012047583

Manufactured in the United States of America

CPSIA Compliance Information: Batch #S13PK5: For Further Information contact Rosen Publishing, New York, New York at 1-800-237-9932

Contents

What Is a Verb?

What would our language be like without verbs? Not very exciting, that's for sure! Verbs are words used to show action or conditions. You cannot say much without using verbs. Some verbs that describe actions are "wish," "seem," and "believe."

Verbs are central to any **sentence**. They tell us what the **noun** in the sentence is doing. Nouns are people, places, or things.

Some verbs that describe conditions are "wish," "seem," and "believe." "Is" describes a condition in the sentence "Jacob is an only child."

4

What verbs might you use to describe what the gymnasts in this photo are doing? Try to come up with several different verbs.

A very simple sentence could be just a noun and a verb. Some verbs are used to help describe action. Both "is" and "running" are verbs in the sentence "Sam is running." "Is" helps describe the action.

FIGURE IT OUT

Can you find the verbs in the following sentences?

Matthew laughs loudly.

The boat is sailing away.

(See answers on p. 22)

The Right Verb

Think of as many verbs as you can. I bet you can come up with a lot! Picking the right word to use is a skill that takes time and practice. It helps to think about exactly what you want to say.

Many verbs describe almost the same action but have small differences. For example, look at the following sentences:

Nathalie jumped over the puddle.

Nathalie hopped over the puddle.

Nathalie leapt over the puddle.

They all describe the same action, but each is slightly different. A hop is a small jump, while a leap is larger.

If you wanted to use a more exact verb than "swims" to describe this dog's action, one good choice might be the word "paddles."

FIGURE IT OUT

How would you describe the differences between the verbs "walk," "strut," and "plod"?

(See answers on p. 22)

7

Regular Verbs

To pick the right form of a verb, you need to know the verb's **subject**. Subjects are nouns or **pronouns** that do a verb's action. Most verbs are **regular**. When a regular verb's subject is "I," "you," "we," or "they," use the base form. This is the form you would find in a **dictionary**. Use the base form with **plural** nouns, too.

Here, a boy splashes in muddy water. You add an "es" to verbs with base forms that end in "ch," "sh," "ss," "x," and "o" when "he," "she," "it," or a singular noun is the subject.

Chart of Forms of "Think"

Subject	Verb Form
I	think
You	think
He	thinks
She	thinks
It	thinks
We	think
They	think

If the subject is "he," "she," "it," or a **singular** noun, add an "s" to the base form. If the base form ends in "y," drop the "y" and add "ies" instead of "s." When writing, always use the correct verb form for the subject. For example, write "they like," not "they likes."

FIGURE IT OUT

What are the correct forms of the verb "share," using "I," "you," he," "she," "it," "we," and "they" as the verb's subjects?

(See answers on p. 22)

Irregular Verbs

Some verbs do not follow the easy pattern that regular verbs do. These verbs are **irregular**. Irregular verbs follow no pattern. You have to learn them with use. One irregular verb that we use every day is the verb "to be." The correct forms of "to be" are "I am," "you are," "he is," "she is," "it is," "we are," and "they are."

Ryan has a dog, and Emily has a cat. The verb "to have" is irregular. If its subject is "he," "she," "it," or a singular noun, the right form is "has."

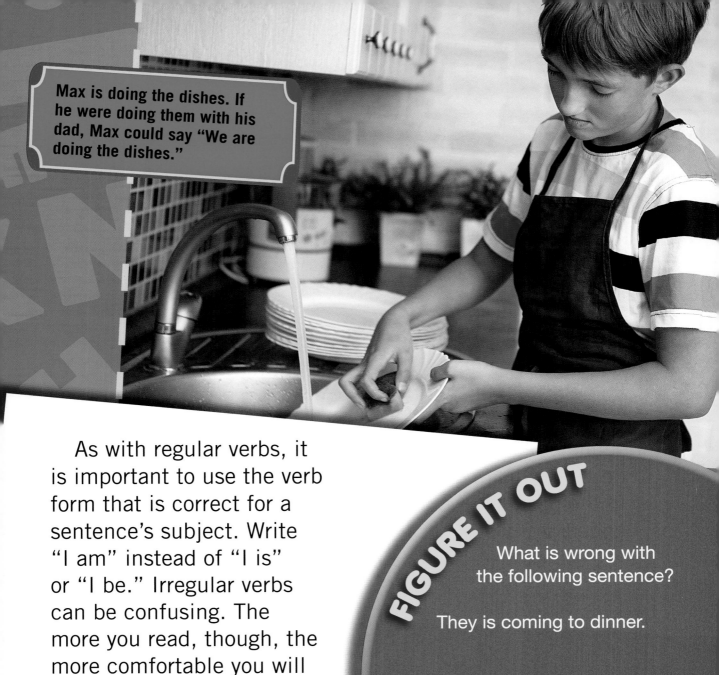

Max is doing the dishes. If he were doing them with his dad, Max could say "We are doing the dishes."

As with regular verbs, it is important to use the verb form that is correct for a sentence's subject. Write "I am" instead of "I is" or "I be." Irregular verbs can be confusing. The more you read, though, the more comfortable you will become with them.

FIGURE IT OUT

What is wrong with the following sentence?

They is coming to dinner.

(See answers on p. 22)

The Past

How do you tell someone what happened yesterday? Verbs can do that! You can use verbs to talk about events that are happening now, events that have happened in the past, or events that will happen in the future.

Verbs used to talk about events that happened in the past take a special form. Usually, you add "ed" to the base form of the verb. As an example, let's take the sentence "My class ends at 3:00." To describe this event as having happened in the past, you would write, "My class ended at 3:00."

Always use the past tense when talking about historical events. For example, you might write, "The Pilgrims sailed to North America on the *Mayflower*."

The Irregular Past

While only a few verbs are irregular when talking about events that are happening now, many more verbs are irregular when talking about events that happened in the past. These can be tricky to learn. However, the more you read, the more you will learn.

"To be" has two past forms. "You," "we," "they," and plural nouns use "were." "I," "he," "she," "it," and singular nouns use "was." That is why you would write, "I was thirsty."

Chart of Past Forms of Irregular Verbs

Irregular Verb	Past Form
Become	Became
Deal	Dealt
Drink	Drank
Get	Got
Know	Knew
Make	Made
Pay	Paid
Ride	Rode
Say	Said
Sit	Sat

There is no easy pattern to the past forms of irregular verbs. You simply have to remember them. For example, "write" is irregular in the past. The correct past form of "write" is "wrote." Another verb that is irregular in the past is "fall." Its past form is "fell." Unfortunately, there are many more!

FIGURE IT OUT

How would you rewrite the following sentence to show that it happened in the past?

I eat toast for breakfast on Monday.

(See answers on p. 22)

The Future

Now let's talk about events that have not yet happened. This future form is a little bit different from the others because it requires extra "helping" words. To talk about a future action, you can use "will" with the base form of the verb, such as "I will start." You can also use a form of "to be," followed by "going to" and the verb's base form, such as "I am going to start."

The two choices have slightly different meanings. Using "will" often means that one is choosing or promising to do something. Using "be going to" often expresses a set plan or something that you think will happen.

Look at the sentence "Jonathan is going to fall, but I will help him get back up." "Is going to fall" and "will help" are both future verb forms.

FIGURE IT OUT

How would you rewrite this sentence so that it is happening in the future?

I called you every day.

(See answers on p. 22)

17

New Verbs

You are bound to come across some unfamiliar verbs while reading. Here's your chance to learn a new verb! One way to figure out the meaning of verbs is to look at the **context**, or words around them.

You can also look closely at the word itself.

To untangle something is to take the tangles, or knots, out of it. "Un" is an affix that makes a word mean the opposite of what it originally meant.

Look at the sentence "The lambs gamboled happily across the grass." The context can help you guess that "to gambol" means to run and jump playfully.

Some unfamiliar words have **roots** or **affixes** with which you might be familiar. Let's say you read the sentence "I hope this problem doesn't recur." Even if you don't know what "recur" means, you might know that the affix "re" means "again." Context could help you guess that "recur" means "happen again."

FIGURE IT OUT

Can you figure out what the italicized word in the following sentence means?

The scientists *unearthed* a huge dinosaur fossil.

(See answers on p. 22)

A Little More Help

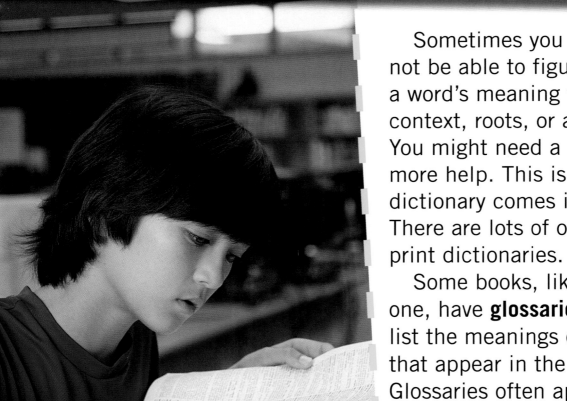

Sometimes you might not be able to figure out a word's meaning through context, roots, or affixes. You might need a little more help. This is when a dictionary comes in handy. There are lots of online and print dictionaries.

Some books, like this one, have **glossaries** that list the meanings of words that appear in the book. Glossaries often appear at the back of a book.

Dictionaries are useful whenever you are reading, writing, or just curious about the meaning of a word you have heard someone use.

Some verbs describe very specific actions. For example, "pitch" means "set up" and is used to describe setting up a tent.

Don't let coming across words that you don't understand get you down. Learning new words is one of the best parts of reading. The more you read, the more you learn!

FIGURE IT OUT

Can you use a dictionary to figure out what the following verbs mean?

endeavor
feign

(See answers on p. 22)

Figure It Out: The Answers

Page 5: The verbs are "laughs," "is," and "sailing."

Page 7: "Walk" is a general word that describes going somewhere by putting one foot in front of the other. "Strut" means to walk in a way that shows off. "Plod" means to walk in a slow, heavy way.

Page 9: The correct forms are: "I share," "You share," "He shares," "She shares," "It shares," "We share," and "They share."

Page 11: The correct verb form would be "are."

Page 13: The sentence should read "The class elected a new president today."

Page 15: It should read "I ate toast for breakfast on Monday."

Page 17: The sentence should be "I will call you every day" or "I am going to call you every day."

Page 19: "Unearthed" means "dug up." The affix "un" means "not." When you unearth something, you make it not in the earth, or ground, any more.

Page 21: To endeavor means to try. To feign means to act falsely or pretend.

Glossary

affixes (A-fiks-ez) Letters or groups of letters that are added to the roots of words to change their meaning.

context (KON-tekst) Words around a word that make that word's meaning clearer.

dictionary (DIK-shuh-ner-ee) A book that lists words alphabetically and explains their meanings.

glossaries (GLAH-suh-reez) Alphabetical lists of words and their meanings.

irregular (ih-REH-gyuh-lur) Not made or done in the usual way.

noun (NOWN) A person, place, idea, state, or thing.

plural (PLUR-el) Having to do with more than one.

pronouns (PRO-nowns) Words that can take the place of nouns.

regular (REH-gyuh-lur) Made or done in the usual way.

roots (ROOTS) The base parts of words.

sentence (SENT-untz) A group of words that forms a complete thought.

singular (SIN-gyuh-lur) Having to do with just one.

subject (SUB-jiktz) The noun or pronoun that carries out the action in a sentence.

Index

Websites

Due to the changing nature of Internet links, PowerKids Press has developed an online list of websites related to the subject of this book. This site is updated regularly. Please use this link to access the list:

www.powerkidslinks.com/cls/verb/